THE LEADER

H. Herchiel Sims

H. Herchiel Sims & Associates
Charleston, West Virginia 1979

First Edition

ISBN: 0-9603772-1-2
Library of Congress Catalog card number 79-92092

To my wife, Elizabeth,
in grateful appreciation for the inspiration
of her unfailing faith and love,
I affectionately dedicate
this book

Preface

AS MACHIAVELLI WROTE "The Prince" for the dictator this book is written for the leader. Francis Schaeffer in his comprehensive book "How Should We Then Live?" states "Machiavelli therefore wrote The Prince advocating firm autocratic rule, because in his view only the dictatorial regime of the 'ideal' prince could push along the cycle of political history; only the exercise of ruthlessness could improve the cycles." The Prince is not an abstract treatise; it is a handbook for the dictator. The aim of "The Leader" is to be a handbook for the leader.

Idealism and realism are the same. This is a key premise for understanding the practicality of leadership in the world today. Most of the world's people have been and are today controlled by dictatorship. The great advances in human development, however, are being made where the people are free to choose leadership as the method for control. Leadership is idealistic and reality is to "improve the cycles." Growing people must be free to choose and Ludwig Von Mises tells us why:

"To choose is to pick one out of two or more possible modes of conduct and to set aside the alternatives. Whenever a human being is in a situation in which various modes of behavior, precluding one another, are open to him, he chooses. Thus life implies an endless sequence of acts of choosing. Action is conduct directed by choices. . . .

"In the strict sense of the term, acting man aims only at one ultimate end, at the attainment of a state of affairs that suits him better than the alternatives. Philosophers and economists describe this undeniable fact by declaring that man prefers what makes him happier to what makes him less happy, that he aims at happiness. . . . Each individual is the only and final arbiter in matters concerning his own satisfaction and happiness.''

A new age is possible through leaders who can harness the power of voluntaryism by seeking to serve humanity as they *set the example.*

This book has been in the making for forty years and is the product of the influence of many people on my life. I would like to thank each individually were it possible. The members of my family, parents, three sisters, six brothers, children and grandchildren are foremost. Fellow workers, soldiers, civic and church leaders have provided inspiration. Help has come from scholars, writers, dictators, leaders, psychologists, economists, philosophers, theologians, historians, statesmen, political leaders who furnished information or influenced my thought process.

I should especially like to acknowledge the influence of Dr. George H. Vick, Leonard Read, Dr. Ernest Ligon, Dwight Eisenhower, Dr. Charles Malik, L. Newton Thomas.

The person who made this work at all possible is my wife, to whom it is dedicated.

Contents

Introduction

AN EON or two ago when one of our cave ancestors was trying to move a very large rock another man *voluntarily* helped him. From this action there dawned the realization that two persons could accomplish a task that one person could not. It was recognized that when two people joined together a power for accomplishment was created that is greater than the separate power of each. This spirit of voluntary cooperation grew until several men were working together under the direction of a person who coordinated the effort. The power of this voluntary coordinated effort was so effective that man for the first time experienced some sense of security. To obtain this voluntary coordinated effort each member gave up certain freedoms. No longer could a man hunt or fish at the time he selected but he must hunt or fish at the time designated by the group leader. This was the price of membership in the group, the price of this collective power. It was voluntary and a person could work within the group, find another group of his choosing or go on his own.

The idea that the greater the number the greater the power prompted a power hungry man to discover that one did not have to depend on voluntaryism, that by coercion and manipulation individuals could be forced to work and obey. Under this stimulus the dictator was born and sought to weld the world into one. This, generally, became the accepted style from antiquity to 1776 when a small group of people put their fortunes and their lives on the line for freedom of the individual. In the same year, 1776, a man by the name of Adam Smith articulated the proposition that voluntary cooperation (i.e. a free market) will produce the greatest amount of goods for the greatest number of people. There can be little doubt that these men and women were the product of another man who was born 1776 years before.

Today in the United States of America there is an opportunity to grasp this heritage and through leadership produce an era of individual freedom, individual opportunity and individual responsibility beyond anything this world has ever known. The potential of dictatorship has been exhausted because free people know they can not grow and perform at their best under coercion. We have moved to the point where only leadership can elicit the voluntary cooperation that is required to advance into a new age, the age of the spirit.

Because of this 200 years of freedom we have in the United States of America the greatest dispersion of power the world has ever seen. The social, economic, political and religious power units can be numbered in the millions. These units have sufficient autonomy to operate on leadership if the spirit of leadership is present. The temptation to try to control by dictatorship is the same today as it has always been i.e. why elect to be a servant when you can be a king!

We define leadership as the art of promoting voluntaryism. It is a method of directing the members of a group towards a goal in such a way as to obtain their obedience, confidence, respect and voluntary cooperation. This art of leading will be discussed under six four letter words.

GOAL   The leader exists for the purpose of achieving a worthy goal.

GROW   Leaders develop through personal growth.

OBEY Obedience is an imperative for accomplishment.

TIME The leader is a producer of qualitative time.

TRUE The leader's theological, economic and political persuasions are compatible.

LOVE Love is the central power and cohesive force of leadership.

I

GOAL

"WORKING WITHOUT a goal is drudgery; a goal without working is a fantasy; working with a goal is victory."

The leader exists for the purpose of accomplishing a *worthy* goal that requires the efforts of two or more people. The leader must know exactly what the goal is and must accept total responsibility for accomplishing it.

Since leadership is not drivership it is dependent on voluntary response from members of the group and requires a goal that elicits obedience to unenforceable law. Establishing a goal is not a democratic process but a

1

leadership decision based on the following:

1. a clear concept on the part of the leader of the goal to be accomplished. If the leader does not know the direction the group is going no one will know.

2. an enthusiasm for the goal that will sustain the leader and imbue the followers with the power to accomplish the goal. Wrote Emerson: "Every great and commanding movement in the annals of the world is the triumph of enthusiasm. Nothing great was ever accomplished without it."

3. a realization that one leads from a base of moral worthiness. The leader must personally exemplify the character traits required to attain the goal.

4. attainment of the goal must contribute to the general welfare and

provide an opportunity for the group member to grow physically, mentally, socially or spiritually.

5. a plan for accomplishing the goal to be used as a test for its practicality. James Allen has put it well "They who have no central purpose in their life fall an easy prey to petty worries, fears, troubles, and self-pitying, all of which lead, just as surely as deliberately planned sins (though by a different route), to failure, unhappiness, and loss, for weakness cannot persist in a power-evolving universe."

6. a realistic understanding of the leadership traits required to achieve the goal.

7. an understanding of the risk involved coupled with a willingness to accept the responsibility to take the risk.

We can look at goals under the two

headings of personal goals and organizational goals. Since our subject is Leadership we are primarily interested in organizational goals. We must recognize, however, that to secure the voluntary compliance required for leadership there must be a direct relationship between the individuals' goals and the organizational goals. A relationship is effected when working toward or achieving the organizational goals contributes directly, or indirectly, to achieving the individuals' goals.

Individuals' goals can be divided into momentary goals, intermediate goals, long term goals and a life goal. Many people have only momentary goals, i.e. they live only for today. Intermediate goals imply that there is a long term goal. For example, the intermediate goals for securing a formal education would be graduating from grade school, high school, college, with the long term goal being a PhD. Receiving a PhD is not worthy of being a life goal. Making the high school football team, just as making a million dollars, is not worthy of being a life goal. We all know people who let intermediate goals end their living because they were never turned on after achieving this lesser goal. A life goal is one that makes a life worth living.

Organizational goals can also be divided into daily goals, intermediate goals, long term goals and primary goal. Envision a service business in which the daily goal is to render a needed service; the intermediate goals are to improve efficiency, reduce cost, improve working conditions and raise wages; the long term goal is to strengthen the organization; the primary goal to make a profit to create capital. We will discuss in Chapter V why to make a profit and create capital is a morally worthy goal.

All members of an organization controlled by leadership should be proud to be a part of that organization. This does not mean, however, that all will be motivated by the same organizational goal. The primary motivation for some members will come from achieving the daily goal while others, especially the leader, will be motivated by accomplishing the long term or primary goal. This individual difference must be recognized if the leader is to maintain a sensitive relationship with workers at all levels.

For successful accomplishment of the organizational goals they must contribute to the leader's goals, they must contribute to the follower's goals. If the organizational goal is incompatible with the leader's personal goal that individual will lack the consistency required of a leader. The same is equally true, from the point of motivation, of the follower. It would be unrealistic to think that the organizational goal is synonymous with either the leader's goals or the follower's goals. The organization and its goals may be only a vehicle through which both the leader and the follower achieve their goals. For example, a long term goal of all individuals should be personal growth. The organizational goal may be to develop a needed and worthwhile business service. If the follower has a goal of personal development and can see by participating in the organizational goal that growth and development to a higher being will result, then motivation is through this feeling of personal growth rather than the actual accomplishment of the organizational goal. One does recognize, however, that it is only through the accomplishment of the organizational goal that one may have the opportunity for achieving one's goal. It is, then, the leader's responsibility to have worthy goals for the organization which can contribute to the follower's personal growth.

It is the leader's responsibility to see that the follower does have established goals. These personal goals well may transcend the organizational goals. We must also recognize that the individual will probably be associated with multiple organizations, i.e. family, religious, civic, business or professional organizations each having goals. If all individual and organizational goals are not homogeneous the individual's effectiveness will be reduced and in some cases destroyed. Goals must be related to purpose. Unless the individual has a feeling of purpose it is unlikely that motivation by any goals will occur. This is to say that one must know where one wants to go with one's life. This is necessary in order to form a consistent motivational base. A leader in selecting the members of the group, would do well to exclude individuals who have not or can not be encouraged to find purposes for their lives. Power is dissipated or multiplied in direct relationship to how each secondary goal relates to the primary goal. A weakening through conflict of interest is obvious when all goals are not homogeneous and contribute to the central goal.

An organization is fragmented when members of the group are striving toward a different goal. An individual is fragmented when participating in the achievement of incompatible goals. The individual who is enthusiastic about setting and achieving personal goals will also be enthusiastic about organizational goals.

Organizations are not ends in themselves but a means to an end. As previously stated the leader and the followers will be involved in many organizations during their life time such as family, religious institutions, government, schools, civic, industrial, business and professional groups. The only worthwhile reason for the existence of any organization is to directly or indirectly fill individual need. This means the organizational goals are subordinate to a worthy life goal. The organization goals may not be subordinate to the individuals' momentary, intermediate or long term goal because achieving the organizational goals can make the greatest contribution to the individuals' life goal.

The leader's long term goal is to grow to the highest potential physically, mentally, socially and spiritually in order to achieve a life goal of service to others. It is by developing physically, mentally, socially and spiritually that the leader has something to give to the leadership position. One can not give away something one does not have i.e. Setting

The Example is the first principle of leadership and is dependent on the leader's continual growth.

The leader seeks for the voluntary response to directives; however, complete voluntary compliance alone, indispensable as it is, is not an automatic guarantee of the health and vitality of leadership. It is only when voluntary compliance is translated into a compulsion to fulfill a distinctive and specific goal that the leader can kindle the urgent enthusiasm and wholehearted commitment which constitutes the bedrock of vigorous group participation.

II

GROW

THE LEADER knows that leadership requires continuous personal growth. To have happy followers they, too, must be growing for happiness is not work, nor pleasure, nor virtue but simply growing physically, mentally, socially, spiritually. Test this for yourself. When you feel out of sorts with everybody and everything, examine your growth pattern. You will probably find that you are in a period of stagnation. You have not been growing physically, mentally, socially and especially spiritually.

It will help if we think of the fully human person as having four bodies i.e. a physical body, a mental body, a social body, and a spiritual body. We can easily observe the great difference between people in their physical bodies. The individual difference in the mental, social and spiritual body is much greater than the individual difference in the physical body. In some people the mental or social or spiritual body may be almost non-existent. Control by leadership is possible only in groups where the leader and group members have the potential and are aware of the presence of these four bodies and have some concept of the steps required to develop them simultaneously.

A person's physical, mental, social and spiritual dimension will determine the positions that person can successfully fill. The leadership position is a continuously expanding opportunity and requires a person who is growing consistently. The leader must be continually growing, also, in

order to lead the follower who is
growing, for leadership releases
human potential, enhances individual dignity and liberates the human
spirit.

It is safe to say that if achieving the
goal does not require the leader and
the followers to grow the goal is not
sufficient for leadership.

Let us discuss physical growth first
because if a person will not accept the
disciplines necessary for physical
growth, the most tangible and easiest
of the four ways we can grow, there is
no reason to expect systematic
growth mentally, socially or spiritually. We should remember that physical growth deals with far more than
size or strength. It deals with appear-
ance, dexterity, coordination, mobil-
ity, sight, hearing, etc.

It is through proper food, proper
exercise and proper rest that we attain our physical growth. What is
proper food, exercise and rest must

be determined by the individual. The leader is ever cognizant of the fact that to maintain control of an expanding range of interests and responsibilities, it is necessary to match them with a growing capacity for self-discipline. This is tough because it is so daily.

A person desirous of physical growth will know exactly the kind and quantity of food he requires to maintain the highest energy level. Knowing the quality of foods and knowing your daily calorie requirement is far more important than knowing what kind of oil and gasoline to put in the car.

Proper rest is, again, a very personal matter but is no great mystery. By experimenting we can determine the amount of sleep and other forms of rest necessary to produce for us the maximum qualitative time.

Thirteen minutes per day is sufficient structured time for most leaders to secure their exercise requirement. The reference here is to the Canadian Air Force exercise plan.

Social development starts with a recognition that togetherness is an essential part of being human. It is one's internalization of the idea that the world was created for all people and that includes "me." We grow socially as we treat others the way we like to be treated. Our growth can be measured by our capacity to do for others as we would have others do for us. The leader grows socially by being a servant to society, that is, by performing tasks that contribute to the welfare, happiness and development of others. The leader is the key to furnishing decent jobs and there is no greater service than providing people with decent work.

Of all the opportunities a leader has for growth, the most rewarding is through contact with genuine leaders, by fellowship with strong, free, successful men and women within the framework of leadership.

Mental growth has been extolled from antiquity. The Greeks believed that all civilization and all progress was based on lifelong enjoyment and improvement of the power of the mind. The mind has to be likened to a computer. What comes out of the mind is what is put into it. "Garbage in—garbage out!" Our mind is programmed by what we look at, what we listen to, what we read, what we watch. We grow mentally by travel, by solving problems, by association with great people in person or through their books, by purposeful association with the follower or, if a follower, with the leader. One of the great blessings derived from being a leader is the stimulant for mental growth. Iron sharpens iron, man sharpens man Proverbs 27:17.

Spiritual development is the growth that keeps the leader from becoming a dictator. Peace is the state that describes a mature person. A person is immature when one's functioning is dependent on the feelings of people around one. Maturity is one's ability to function unaffected by praise or criticism. Peace is a product of maturity. By seeking God's will the leader is affirming that all leaders have a leader. This raises the leader above the destructive forces of pride, covetousness, lust, anger, gluttony, envy and produces in the leader prudence, justice, temperance, fortitude, faith, hope and love. The leader grows spiritually by devoting some time each day to reading the Bible, to prayer, and to worship.

For spiritual fitness the leader exercises the trust muscle.

III

OBEY

THE LEADER exists for the purpose of accomplishing a *worthy* goal, and obedience is an imperative for accomplishment. Only the immature thinks of obeying as being virtuous or for the purpose of pleasing God or any earthly power. Many peoples' attitude toward obedience is that they are serving another person's good by obeying rather than understanding that one is in service to one's self when obeying the basic laws, rules or regulations that are necessary to attain the goal. For example, many people believe that to obey the Commandments of God is in service to Him. To the contrary! Not one Commandment has been given that is not for the purpose of serving the individual and providing for that individual a full and happy life. When persons commit themselves voluntarily to any endeavor, they obey the rules necessary to achieve the goal because this is the way to success. They are not obeying the rules because someone wants them to obey. It is the very immature individual who rebels at obeying those laws, rules or regulations that are proper for the purpose of establishing a better society. It is only through that better society that a social individual can have the opportunity for self fulfillment.

We obey because it is the only way we can win. Each in his own way desires success. If we want to be successful, we identify and obey the laws, the principles, the regulations that will bring success.

For our thinking, we will divide these laws and principles into three categories: natural law or conformity to the order in the universe; social law or conformity to the established social order; project principles or conformity to that which is necessary to successfully maintain a home, business, profession or any activity requiring the association of two or more persons.

Our priority for obedience must be from natural law to social law to project principles. This is to say that to be a leader we must first obey the natural law; second, the social law and then the project principles. What if the social law is in conflict with the natural law or the project principles? Leadership requires freedom to choose. Without the right to choose i.e. unnecessary restriction by the social order, the individual cannot experience the blessings of leadership and must suffer under the limitations of dictatorship. Fortunately in the United States of America we live in a social structure that can support the leader as a parent, entrepreneur, labor organizer, cleric. However, we should recognize that limitations placed on leadership by government actions curtail the individual's right to choose and hampers leadership development. This will be dealt with in Chapter V TRUE.

One of the greatest of all paradoxes is that *all our freedoms stem from obedience.*

The natural law, the social law and the project principles can be thought of as planks of a ship that keep us afloat as we voyage through life. Without these supports we have nothing on which to travel and we dare not venture forth. These laws cannot be broken; we merely break ourselves against them.

The leader is steeped in knowledge of the natural law and seeks continually to understand and apply these unchangeable laws to the daily task. It is from this foundation that the leader will recognize the validity of and operate within the social law and project principles. The leader does not think of laws and principles as burdens but as blessings that make all things possible. They are the essential part of the leader's character.

We have said that to win one must obey. Consider the objective as "good health." We know that to have good health we must have proper food, proper exercise, proper rest. It is not difficult for each individual to know what constitutes proper food, exercise and rest however, it is a daily problem to implement this knowledge. When we understand why it is so easy to recognize how other people are losing their freedom by their failure to properly eat, exercise and rest we may understand one of the great lessons on obedience. Basically our problem is that we want to win but we do not want to give up a momentary pleasure. The child is interested in only the moment; the mature individual foregoes the momentary pleasure when it interferes with achieving the goal, a higher joy.

All organized efforts require obedience from the participants to accomplish the mission. In this premise there is no difference between dictatorship and leadership. Obedience to enforceable law can easily be obtained by a strong dictator and, most easily of all, from a timorous people. The leader seeks obedience beyond enforceable law to *unenforceable* law. An example of *unenforceable* law would be the actions of the men aboard the Titanic. No law compelled them to give women and children first right to the lifeboat. If they had not made this commitment, no civil law would have been invoked to punish them. They obeyed a greater law that is unenforceable. You can buy a person's presence at a given place for a given length of time, but you cannot force from the person creativity or any of the unenforceable qualities that contribute to accomplishing the goal.

Outward obedience is by no means all that is desirable in the work situation. It is the inner attitude that really matters. A person with great skills and poor work attitudes is less productive than a person with adequate skills and good attitudes. The leader will attract individuals with right attitudes and will maintain the atmosphere within the organization that is conducive to sustain right attitudes.

Right attitudes are reflected by the individual's actions on the job, such as initiative, diligence, enthusiasm for the work, devotion to duty, honest day's work. These, of course, are other unenforceables on the job.

When we get to the real core of this

attitude concept of obedience we recognize that the example of right attitudes stems from the character of the leader. If the leader does not reflect right attitudes, he or she will either turn people with good attitudes into people with bad attitudes, or the people with good attitudes will leave the organization.

Obedience involves the decision making process. The goal to be achieved will determine the essential to be obeyed. First, if we are to know what to obey we must know the goal we are trying to achieve. Second, we must know the laws, principles, rules and regulations that must be obeyed to accomplish the goal. Third, we must decide if we are willing to obey those imperatives that are necessary to achieve the goal. This means, very simply, that we are committing ourselves to do certain things and to give up doing other things. The choice we make will determine how we will use our time. How we use our time will determine the goals we reach and the goals we attain will determine who we are. By foreknowledge of the commitments, through the decision process, the leader is not surprised when it is necessary to forego worthwhile and pleasing activities. To accomplish the goal may mean giving up not only pleasures but friends and prestigious position. Obedience is most difficult, if not impossible, for a person who cannot make and carry out tough decisions.

The leader knows that to maintain control of an expanding range of interests one must match these with a growing capacity to discipline one's self. The normal tendency is for a person to relax self discipline as one becomes successful. We often do not have the pressures continue that caused us to do the things we should do, and did do, to arrive at our present position. The higher the position the greater the temptations become. All kinds of power and pleasure temptation are presented to the successful. Once compromised few escape as did Ulysses from Circe. The constant prayer of the leader is "lead me not into temptation but deliver me from evil." The leader knows that the greatest temptation of all comes when the position of power permits the establishment of rules and regulations. This is the point where many a leader has succumbed to dictatorship. The power to obey one's self is the greatest source of power a leader can have and there is no likelihood that leadership is possible without self control.

At this point we should discuss RHIP. Rank has its privilege. We cannot lead nor can we expect those under us to lead unless they have privileges in relationship to their responsibilities. A better way to interpret RHIP is to say that *responsibility*

has its privilege. The leader should
be accorded and must graciously accept all privileges that will

1. save time

2. protect from harm

3. foster good health

4. contribute to manner and bear-
   ing

5. save the leader's energy

6. help make decisions

7. alleviate irritations.

The leader refuses all privileges that
do not contribute to achieving the
goal.

The enlightened followers, and
they will not remain followers long
unless they are enlightened, know
the importance of the leader to their
cause. To the followers the leader's
welfare is second only to accomplish-

ing the goal because the leader is the primary power through which the goal will be obtained and maintained. As pointed out in Chapter I GOAL the follower's welfare is tied to accomplishing the goal. Attaining the goal is not only important to the leader, it is of concern to all members in the organization.

The leader must have knowledge of and be subject to a great many more laws and project principles than the follower. This means that the leader is far more subject to obedience than any other member of the organization.

To lead one must be capable of standing firmly upon his own feet in the world of daily work, temptation and trial. The leader must be able to bear the wear and tear of life as it is. Cloistered virtues do not count for much when we are dealing with the control of a work force through leadership.

It is the leader who determines the laws and project principles that are germane to accomplishing the goal. The leader has no right to expect obedience to any law or principle that is not a requirement for achieving the goal.

The leader will, when possible, enlighten members of the group as to why obedience to a law or principle is required to accomplish the goal. Sometimes leaders cannot explain the reason for the law or principle because their own acceptance is not based on personal feeling but on *faith* in that law or principle. Often when teaching instrument flying the instructor will induce vertigo and then turn the controls over to the student. Invariably the student's "feel" is contrary to the instrument. He reacts wrongly for the student's tendency is to believe personal feelings instead of instrument reading. The student must learn to operate against feelings in obedience to instrument reading. If he doesn't he will destroy himself.

Leaders know that they must accept fundamental laws and principles and apply them, when possible, even though at the moment it may appear expeditious to follow their feelings and disobey. The follower must have faith in the leader and be willing to accept the governing laws and principles to achieve the goal. The proof comes when the student pilot lands safely at the destination or the organization achieves the goal. Success breeds faith in obedience to laws and principles and in the leader.

The leader must attract followers who will obey those things that are necessary in order to achieve the goal.

This does not mean that the followers must be obedient to all of the ideals or customs that the leader adheres to or thinks is important.

This premise will keep the leader

from being involved in the individual's life or choices where it is not necessary to achieve the goal.

This is saying, in effect, that the leader must have firmly in mind the obedience requirement that is related to the goal. A careful definition of the goal or what is to be accomplished is essential in sorting out the obedience framework.

A requirement as to grooming or dress code is a clear example. In certain situations the length of a person's hair could be a valid concern of the leader. The length of a person's hair could either help or be a deterrent if the individual occupies a position that requires communication with others. Where an individual's work is performed in solo, such as Einstein, the length of the hair may be of no concern and the capable leader will not be denied the service of this person because of personal likes or dislikes.

A person's attitude toward obedience should be determined when selecting the person for membership on the team. Also the obedience requirements of the job should be a part of the pre-selection process. If a person cannot perform satisfactorily without direct supervision that person should not be employed for unsupervised duties.

A person must earn the right to be led as much as one must earn the right to lead. If a person does not develop the attitudes that will let one voluntarily comply the only alternative is for one to be subject to the arbitrary whim of a dictator. The leader simply cannot condone those individuals who will not voluntarily do those things that are necessary in order to accomplish a worthwhile goal.

The match then between the leader and the follower comes about when each has freely accepted the task to be performed and, without pressure from the top, the individual voluntarily responds to the need of the task.

When dealing with the idea of obedience, it is far more important that leaders understand and program themselves to obey than it is that they study ways and means of gaining obedience from other people.

The temptation when we are trying to effect a practical approach to obedience is to think in terms of how we can get others to obey.

If Albert Schweitzer is correct, "Example is not the main thing in influencing; it is the only thing" then our own obedience will do more to elicit obedience from others than any other single thing we can do.

The internalization of obedience leads us to a frame of mind that we obey even the simplest rule whenever possible. For example, the amber stop light is a signal that we should stop rather than a signal that we should speed up to see if we can beat the red light. Knowing this we program the proper response. This simple type of obedience will keep us from the destructive effect of obeying only the enforceable laws.

We search for truth in order to obey that truth. When we discover *Truth* and fail to obey that truth we are like a person who finds a precious stone and tosses it into the ocean. We may never recognize that truth again.

IV

TIME

FOR EVERY day of our life all are given the same quantity of time: 86,400 seconds. The leader knows that one second of qualitative time is worth more than 86,399 seconds of wasted time.

The leader is a producer of qualitative time. The leader turns quantity time into quality time for himself and for the followers.

Qualitative time is time that contributes to:

1. the leader's growth physically, mentally, socially and spiritually

2. the follower's growth physically, mentally, socially and spiritually

3. the achievement of a worthy goal.

We must be ever mindful that a leader exists for the purpose of achieving a worthy organizational goal. The growth or development of the leader and the follower is necessary to achieve goals. As stated before, if achieving the goal does not require the leader and the follower to grow the goal is not sufficient for leadership.

The leader produces qualitative time through commitment, constancy to purpose, growth, freedom, discipline, risk taking, allocation of time, establishing a quiet period, eliminating unnecessaries, timeliness and by planned association. Each will be touched on in the following paragraphs.

Commitment The most important way the leader can produce qualitative time for the organization is by personal commitment to accomplishing a certain worthy goal within a definite time limit and to encourage the followers to have responsible commitment to goals. Time seems magically tailored to our commitments. However, the leader knows that too many commitments amount virtually to none, so will avoid being over committed or over committing the followers.

Constancy to Purpose There is more wasted time from incompleted projects than from any other single action. It is the easiest way to destroy what would have been qualitative time. A leader will systematically determine the progress being made on all organization projects and will keep the followers informed as to purpose and progress.

Growth   An individual's capacity to use a skill, make decisions, promote harmony, be responsible and direct the work of others is increased by personal growth. One's capacity to perform will determine how much time it takes to accomplish a task. Even more important, a person's capacity for accomplishment will determine whether the task can be achieved. The leader will consider it a primary responsibility to assure personal growth and the followers' growth.

Freedom   The individual differences in people demand the maximum freedom possible for the greatest efficiency. Individuals will differ as to what they do best, when they can work best, how they can best perform, and where the work can best be done. The leader will promote the greatest freedom commensurate with required structure.

Discipline The importance of discipline to qualitative time is clearly stated by Elton Trueblood "Acceptance of discipline is the price of freedom. The pole vaulter is not free to go over the high bar except as he disciplines himself rigorously day after day. The freedom of the surgeon to use his drill to cut away the bony structure, close to a tiny nerve without severing it, arises from a similar discipline. It is doubtful if excellence in any field comes in any other way. John Milton was revealing something of his own creative power when he wrote, 'There is not that thing in the world of more grave and urgent importance, throughout the whole life of man, than is discipline.' " The starting point for implementing this way of producing qualitative time is to implement the simple but demanding daily disciplines of proper food, exercise and rest.

Establish A Quiet Period   An hour of uninterrupted time can be worth several hours of interrupted time when the work is thinking, planning, getting organized. The leader can increase personal qualitative time by a quiet hour and also by establishing a quiet hour for the followers. The unit quiet hour is when everyone in the unit will refrain from interrupting other members of the unit except in case of an emergency. The unit quiet hour must be voluntary for each member and must have the leader's cooperation and support. All participants are expected to be at their work place for this quiet period.

Eliminating Unnecessaries   Isaac Newton who was moderate in all his habits was once asked why he did not smoke. He replied, "Because I do not want to acquire any new necessities." The less of our time we spend on unnecessaries the more time we will have for those things that give us qualitative time.

Timeliness There is a most productive time for every endeavor. Planting corn out of season is a waste of time as is manufacturing a product when the market is not right. "He was successful because he knew when to act" is a familiar and an accepted adage. It is more difficult, if not impossible, to do a thing before the time is right. In most cases when something must be done the best time is the earliest possible time.

Planned Association Let us listen to Charles Malik on the importance of our associates. "How do we become true and good, happy and genuine, joyful and free? Never by magic, never by chance, never by sitting and waiting, but only by getting in touch with good, true, happy, genuine human beings, only by seeking the company of the strong and the free, only by catching spontaneity and freedom from those who are themselves spontaneous and free." The leader will seek opportunities for intercourse with "genuine human beings" and will provide this qualitative time for the followers.

You can develop a better understanding of qualitative time by making a list of those activities you believe produce qualitative time for you such as family time, earning time, study time, creative time, planning time, supervising time, worship time, leisure time, socializing time, rest time, etc. As near as you can in 15 minute periods set forth how you spent your time this day, this week. After each block of time place a Q for qualitative time or a W for wasted time. On those blocks of time where you place a Q indicate by a WK work time, L leisure time, W worship time. Are you satisfied with your qualitative time picture? Most of our qualitative time pictures are easy to improve. Keep this first picture and make a second picture next week. Work on producing qualitative time and you will be amazed at your increase in joy and productivity.

The biggest problem with most of us is the quality of our lives. How we use our time will determine the goals we reach and the goals we attain will determine who we are. The quality of life can be measured by determining the amount and quality of our qualitative time. Whatever gets your time gets you. The leader seeks qualitative time.

V

TRUE

What is TRUE? There is no god or there is one all wise, all powerful, infinite, eternal God whose nature is love?

What is TRUE? The human race can evolve to the highest potential through an economic system based on communism or individualism?

What is TRUE? The greatest good can be achieved through a totalitarian or a limited governmental system?

Since the foundation of leadership is moral worthiness the leader's and the follower's theological, economic and political persuasion must be based on that which is morally right. Morality is truth in action and points to the first and most important principle of leadership: *set the example.*

To set the example the leader must be consistent in his thoughts and actions. To be consistent the leader's theological, economic and political faith must be compatible or the leader will act against the purpose served. Since the leader's source of power is derived from the follower's obedience to unenforceable laws the theological, economic and political system that allows for the greatest freedom for the leader and the follower is the best framework for leadership. We must not lose sight of the truth that all freedom stems from obedience. One's theological position is preeminent because it is the basis for choosing economic and political faith. Faith is a kind of divine insight which helps one to apprehend unseen reality. It can grasp that which lies beyond our sense and reason i.e. the practicality of freedom for the individual. Faith is required for understanding and supporting the economic and political as well as the theological position one will live by.

Leadership's Theological Persuasion:

The leader knows that the only way to consistently maintain the moral foundation required of a leader is to draw on the Infinite Power. Through obedience to God one is free to use God given time and talent in the role of a servant to accomplish a worthy goal within a structure that

1. promotes individual responsibility

2. elicits voluntary cooperation

3. releases human potential

4. liberates the human spirit

5. enhances individual dignity

6. emphasizes the importance of the individual.

The leader's answer to What is TRUE? is: an abiding faith in one, all wise, all powerful, infinite, eternal God whose nature is love.

Leadership's Economic Persuasion:

Is it a communistic economic system (Socialism) or an individualistic economic system (Capitalism) that correlates with a leader's theological system? By communistic we mean government ownership of all natural resources and tools of production through which the economy is controlled by fixing production, wages and prices. Individualistic is defined as an economic system based on the individual ownership of natural resources and tools of production (the right of private property) and allowing a free market to determine production, wages and prices.

The dominant question: Which of the two systems, individualism or communism, warrants a higher productivity of human effort to improve people's standard of living?

By answering the following questions the leader can determine the economic system that is consistent with the leader's theological position.

1. Which system promotes individual responsibility?
   Communistic   Individualistic

2. Which system elicits voluntary cooperation?
   Communistic   Individualistic

3. Which system releases human potential?
   Communistic   Individualistic

4. Which system liberates the human spirit?
   Communistic   Individualistic

5. Which system enhances individual dignity?

   Communistic   Individualistic

6. Which system emphasizes the importance of the individual?

   Communistic   Individualistic

The leader's answer to What is TRUE economically is a firm faith in the individual, reinforced by statistical knowledge on productivity.

"Old Mother Hubbard went to the
   cupboard
To get her poor dog a bone
And when she got there the
   cupboard was bare
And so the poor dog had none."

The leader as an idealist is a realist so an inward economic sense tells the leader that you cannot consume what is not produced. Productivity flows naturally from a free individual who can profit through frugality, creativity, initiative, diligence and devotion to duty. Substitute a communist system which requires coercion for control, and creativity, initiative, diligence and devotion to duty are destroyed. Any frugality is a matter of necessity and is not a result of self-discipline.

Individualism, capitalism, free enterprise are all the same and require two restraints. First, a spiritual restraint which comes from worshipping a just and loving God. Second, governmental restraints since all people will not at all times voluntarily accept the spiritual restraint. Unless men are motivated by moral principles they will seek power and wealth by pursuing practices which demoralize and weaken other people.

Leadership's Political Persuasion:

It is from the realization that anarchy destroys all freedom and the totalitarian state is the end result of dictatorship that the leader works out his faith in a limited government philosophy under God that emphasizes

> Freedom for the individual
> Opportunity for all
> Responsibility of citizenship

The leader cannot be passive in his political faith since the governmental system will determine to a large degree where leadership can be practiced i.e. there is little opportunity for leadership in any endeavor where the government determines service, sets goals, orders research, fixes salaries, selects personnel and determines power structure. The totalitarian state is to dictatorship what the limited government philosophy is to leadership.

The limited government philosophy is far more than limiting government power in certain areas. It is excluding governmental control from areas such as religion. Since the very

nature of government requires autonomy it is most difficult to limit
government within an area. Whatever area the government is allowed
to enter it can control or destroy
through its police power and its ap-
paratus of coercion and compulsion.
By limited government we do not
mean a weak governmental system
but a government with the power to
fulfill its essential responsibilities to
maintain the peace. Government can
be limited through a democratic process that permits the citizenry to
select their ruler and a constitution
that limits the area of government
intervention plus guarantees certain
rights to the minorities as well as the
majorities. It is a government with a
constitution that limits law.

Atheism, communism and the totalitarian state form the consistent
theological, economic and political
position for dictatorship. The dictator
cannot afford to share power even

with God much less ordinary mortals.

The leader whose aim is purpose not power can move from leader to follower to leader without any loss of ego. This is possible because of a theology that puts God first, an economic philosophy that recognizes the individual as the most important unit of society and a political position that protects the individual from autocratic control.

In Chapter III OBEY we said that fortunately in the USA we live in a social structure that can support the leader as a parent, entrepreneur, labor organizer, cleric, etc. This is true because of the theological, economic and political base in the USA and will remain true so long as this country has a power structure of real leaders dedicated to the idealism expressed thus: "I pledge allegiance to the Flag of the United States of America and to the Republic for which it stands; one nation under

God, indivisible, with liberty and justice for all."

The dictator must consistently protect and extend his autocratic base. The right to lead must be continually protected and extended by all leaders in a free society through the example they set in their theological, economic and political activities.

" . . . whatever is true . . . think about these things." Philippians 4:8

VI

LOVE

LOVE IS the central power of leadership. Volumes could be filled with testimonies from the great, the powerful, the wise on the power of love.

Napoleon Bonaparte—emperor, military genius, contributor to French law: "You are amazed at the conquests of Alexander. But here is a conqueror who appropriates to his own advantage, who incorporates with himself not a nation but the human race. Alexander, Caesar, Charlemagne and myself founded empires; but upon what did we rest the creations of our genius? Upon force. Jesus alone founded His empire upon love; and at this hour millions of men would die for him."

Will Durant—historian, philosopher: "My final lesson of history is the same as that of Jesus. You may think that's a lot of lollipop, but just try it. Love is the most practical thing in the world."

This thorough scholar, who has spent 70 years studying and writing about the world as it is, unequivocably states that love is the most practical thing in the world. What is love? What do we mean by love in leadership? We are presented with a problem in semantics that is clarified for us by the Greeks who gave us four words for the one.

Eros meaning sensual love, romantic love, and love for those who have something which we lack, as the Romans loved the various Roman gods.

Storge refers to family affection, great fondness.

Philos is the love of friend for

friend; brotherly love; fraternal; liking to be with one.

Agapē love is for all mankind. It is not a liking kind of love but a concern for another's well-being.

In certain relationships two or more of these loves may be present. We would hope that all four loves would be present in a marriage. Philos and agapē may be present in an industrial organization.

When we speak of love in leadership we are talking about agapē, the only love that is not emotional and the one that the leader can order to be present in his life. Agapē can be analyzed in three elements: recognition, consideration, care. You can order yourself to recognize that there are other people in the world besides yourself, you can order yourself to consider the interests of others as well as your own, you can order yourself to care for the well-being of others. This agapē has been cited as the power that prompted the writers of the Declaration of Independence to say that all people are created equal in that they are endowed with the right to life, liberty and the pursuit of happiness. This agapē is what guarantees the dignity of the individual.

Through agapē love the leader develops the capacity, the power for leadership. It is indispensable for control as Leo Tolstoi said "The trouble begins because men sometimes think that you can handle people without love and you cannot. You can handle things without love. You can carve wood and hammer iron without it, but you cannot deal with people in this way. People are like bees. If you handle bees roughly, either they will get hurt or you will get hurt."

This does not mean that the leader is a patsy, illustrated by incidents in the lives of three of America's greatest leaders who epitomized agapē love. George Washington ordered the mistreatment of British prisoners of war when he found it was necessary to keep the British from abusing American prisoners of war. General Thomas Gage ignored Washington's plea that American prisoners be treated under the prisoner of war rule. General Gage was treating the American prisoners as traitors to their country. Washington ordered that the British prisoners of war should be treated in the same manner as the British treated the Americans. This brought the result that Washington hoped for as the British stopped abusing American war prisoners.

In December of 1848 Abraham Lincoln wrote a letter to his step-brother replying to the step-brother's request to borrow $80. This letter is a masterpiece of compassion coupled with the refusal to send the money because the money would not help this brother. This, in part, is what Lincoln said,

"You are not lazy, and still you are an idler. I doubt whether since I saw you, you have done a good whole day's work, in any one day. You do not very much dislike to work; and still you do not work much, merely because it does not seem to you that you could get much for it. This habit of needlessly wasting time is the whole difficulty; and it is vastly important to you, and still more so to your children, that you should break this habit. It is more important to them, because they have longer to live, and can keep out of an idle habit before they are in it, easier than they can get out after they are in." The letter went ahead to offer his brother a work incentive plan. These words of Lincoln show the realism of love "I want it to be said of me, by those who knew me best, that wherever I found a thorn, I plucked it up, and planted a rose, wherever I felt a rose would grow."

Robert E. Lee who has been crowned by history for his love gave his Colonel Mosby permission to retaliate by hanging three and shooting three Federal soldiers. The circumstance: George Custer under General Sheridan had at Front Royal two weeks before summarily hanged three Virginia youths and had attached notes to their bodies saying "This will be the fate of Mosby and all his men." How could Robert E. Lee, this man of love, approve taking the lives of two for one! He said, "A dreadful business but those people must be taught the rules of warfare." Federal General Grant ordered Sheridan to cease such violations of the rules of war and Custer was reprimanded. These examples are given to dispel the idea that love destroys the expectation for obedience. Washington, Lincoln and Lee are ideals because they were realists. Idealism is realism.

The father who says "I cannot love my children all the time because I must see that they obey" has pinpointed very well the irrationalization of those who separate love and truth. Agapē love is tough minded because this is the only way a person having the responsibility of leadership can be successful as a leader. A leader will neither tolerate abuse of the followers nor condone disobedience in the followers.

The essence of agapē love and the traits of the leader are inseparably linked in the Beatitudes and provide a life plan for leadership development.

Happy are the poor in spirit = humility = the leader is aware of his finiteness and place in the universe.

Happy are the pure in heart = servant = the leader's dominant purpose is to serve mankind.

Happy are they who hunger and thirst for righteousness = realist = the leader is continually seeking for truth.

Happy are the meek = obedience = the leader has confidence in and respect for truth.

Happy are they that mourn = sensitive = the leader is sensitive to the needs of others.

Happy are the merciful = justice = the leader is determined to give every one the opportunity for happiness and success.

Happy are the peacemakers = magnanimous = the leader resolves the conflicts within and between people.

Happy are they who are persecuted for righteousness sake = courage = the leader wills to serve humanity even in the face of poverty, injustice and unwarranted punishment.

Love is the cohesive factor in leadership. It is that which binds leader to follower, follower to leader, and follower to follower. As we said earlier, the follower must earn the right to leadership as much as the leader earns the right to lead. The follower, like the leader, can order agapē love, the power that binds the unit together. This agapē love is the dynamo, the great transformer, turning ambition into aspiration, selfishness into service, greed into gratitude, getting into giving and demands into dedication.

Words, after all, are pale ghosts and must be fleshed out in the example of the leader. In the American dream the word "independence" was a pale ghost until it was fleshed out in the mind, heart and hands of a Jefferson. Agapē love must be fleshed out in the mind, heart and hands of the leader as he carries out the responsibilities of leading whether it be in parenting, in government, in industry, in business, in labor, or in the professions. For a person without agapē love to be a leader would be like a deaf person becoming a music critic.

We shall close with the words of Charles Malik "For that which you really believe to be true and human and universal you will want to share with others, you cannot keep under a bushel. . . . Only he therefore who feels with humanity, who is at one with all conditions of men, who is insufficient and incomplete without them, who is not protected and separated from them, can help them and lead them and love them and be loved by them."

May God be your leader.